TODO ACERCA DEL OTOÑO/ALL ABOUT FALL

Los espantapájaros/
Scarecrows

Revised Edition

por/by Calvin Harris

Traducción/Translation: Dr. Martín Luis Guzmán Ferrer
Editor consultor/Consulting Editor: Dra. Gail Saunders-Smith

CAPSTONE PRESS
a capstone imprint

Pebble Plus is published by Capstone Press,
1710 Roe Crest Drive, North Mankato, Minnesota, 56003
www.mycapstone.com

Library of Congress Cataloging-in-Publication Data is available on the Library of Congress website.
ISBN: 978-1-5157-6187-7 (paperback)
ISBN: 978-1-5157-6188-4 (ebook pdf)

Editorial Credits
Sarah L. Schuette, editor; Katy Kudela, bilingual editor; Adalín Torres-Zayas, Spanish copy editor;
    Veronica Bianchini, designer

Photo Credits
Dreamstime: Ken Cole, Cover; Capstone Studio: Karon Dubke, 1, 5, 9, 11, 13, 15, 17, 19, 21;
Shutterstock: klerik78, 7

Pebble Plus thanks Emma Krumbee's in Belle Plaine, Minnesota, and the Minnesota Landscape Arboretum in
    Chaska, Minnesota, for the use of their locations during photo shoots.

Note to Parents and Teachers

The Todo acerca del otoño/All about Fall set supports national science standards related
to changes during the seasons. This book describes and illustrates scarecrows in fall in
both English and Spanish. The images support early readers in understanding the text.
The repetition of words and phrases helps early readers learn new words. This book also
introduces early readers to subject-specific vocabulary words, which are defined in the
Glossary section. Early readers may need assistance to read some words and to use the
Table of Contents, Glossary, Internet Sites, and Index sections of the book.

Printed and bound in the USA.
009969R

Table of Contents

Tabla de contenidos

Fall Is Here

It's fall. The weather is getting cooler. Scarecrows stand in the cornfields.

Llegó el otoño

Es otoño. El tiempo se pone más fresco. Los espantapájaros están de pie en los maizales.

Scarecrows guard fields and gardens. They scare birds away from plants and crops.

Los espantapájaros vigilan los campos y los jardines. Asustan a los pájaros para que se alejen de las plantas y cultivos.

Scarecrow Parts

Scarecrows look like people.
They wear shirts and pants
stuffed with yellow straw.

Las partes del espantapájaros

Los espantapájaros se parecen
a las personas. Usan camisas
y pantalones rellenos de
paja amarilla.

8

Scarecrows wear
boots on their
straw feet.

Los espantapájaros
tienen botas en sus
pies de paja.

10

Scarecrows wear hats
on their orange
pumpkin heads.

Los espantapájaros usan
sombreros en sus cabezas
de calabazas anaranjadas.

Fun with Scarecrows

People use scarecrows
as fun fall decorations.

A divertirse con los espantapájaros

Las personas usan
espantapájaros como
divertidos adornos
de otoño.

People dress scarecrows
in funny ways.

Las personas visten a
los espantapájaros de
maneras muy divertidas.

16

People wear scarecrow
costumes on Halloween.

En *Halloween*, los niños
se ponen disfraces
de espantapájaros.

18

Other Signs of Fall

Scarecrows are a sign of fall.
What are other signs
that it's fall?

Otras señales del otoño

Los espantapájaros son una
señal del otoño. ¿Qué otras
señales hay que ya es otoño?

Glossary

decoration — an object that makes a place or another object prettier or more exciting

field — an area of land where crops grow

guard — to protect or keep watch over a person or a place

Halloween — a fall holiday where people dress up in costumes and go out trick-or-treating

straw — the dried stalks of field crops; straw usually has a yellow color.

weather — the conditions outside at a certain time and place

Glosario

el adorno — objeto que hace que un lugar u otro objeto sean más bonitos o emocionantes

el campo — superficie de tierra donde crecen cultivos

Halloween — día de fiesta en otoño cuando las personas se disfrazan y salen a pedir regalos, y si no se los dan responden con una broma

la paja — los tallos secos de los cultivos del campo; la paja generalmente es de color amarillo.

el tiempo — las condiciones a la intemperie a cierta hora y lugar

vigilar — proteger o cuidar a una persona o un lugar

Internet Sites

FactHound offers a safe, fun way to find educator-approved Internet sites related to this book.

Here's what you do:

1. Visit *www.facthound.com*
2. Choose your grade level.
3. Begin your search.

This book's ID number is 9781429632638.

FactHound will fetch the best sites for you!

Index

Sitios de Internet

FactHound te brinda una forma segura y divertida de encontrar sitios de Internet relacionados con este libro y aprobados por docentes.

Lo haces así:

1. Visita *www.facthound.com*
2. Selecciona tu grado escolar.
3. Comienza tu búsqueda.

El número de identificación de este libro es 9781429632638.

¡FactHound buscará los mejores sitios para ti!

Índice